CW01149948

Original title:
Sunbeam Shadows

Copyright © 2024 Creative Arts Management OÜ
All rights reserved.

Author: Penelope Hawthorne
ISBN HARDBACK: 978-9916-90-748-1
ISBN PAPERBACK: 978-9916-90-749-8

Shadows of Joy

In laughter's echo, shadows play,
Beneath the trees where children sway.
Their fleeting smiles, a soft embrace,
In moments lost, we find our place.

In twilight hues, we chase the light,
As whispers dance in fading night.
With open hearts, we learn to sing,
While shadows tell of joyous spring.

Reflections in Gloom

In corners dark, our secrets dwell,
A heavy heart, a silent shell.
The echoes linger, time stands still,
As shadows grasp and bend the will.

Through windows fogged, we search for grace,
Yet find ourselves in lost embrace.
The twilight shadows weave their tale,
In twilight's grasp, the hopes grow frail.

Secrets Beneath the Canopy

The forest whispers ancient lore,
Where every branch hides tales of yore.
In emerald hues, the silence swells,
With secrets dark the woodland tells.

Beneath the boughs, the shadows weave,
A tapestry for those who believe.
With every step, the stories flow,
In hidden paths, the glimmers glow.

Celestial Gradients

In twilight's grasp, the colors blend,
A canvas vast that knows no end.
Stars emerge in whispered tones,
As night unveils its silent thrones.

The moonlight bathes the world below,
In gradients of soft, silver glow.
Each heartbeat echoes cosmic flight,
In endless dance of day to night.

Mosaics of Light

Fragments of color, a dance in the sky,
Whispers of dawn as the shadows comply.
Each hue a story, each shade a song,
Crafting the canvas where dreams belong.

Glints on the water, they shimmer and play,
Reflecting the hopes of the coming day.
Patterns unravel, a tapestry bright,
Weaving the magic of moments in light.

Eclipsed Illumination

In shadows we wander, the light fades away,
An eclipse of the heart on this tranquil bay.
Silhouettes linger as thoughts intertwine,
In the hush of the twilight, our souls align.

Yet glimmers remain, a spark in the gloom,
Whispers of laughter still weave through the room.
Within every darkness, a promise to shine,
In eclipsed illumination, your hand in mine.

Luminescent Reveries

Dreams of the night, they shimmer and flow,
Painting the silence with a soft, radiant glow.
Stars weave their stories, a dance up above,
Echoes of wishes, the night sings of love.

In twilight's embrace, our fantasies rise,
With luminescent whispers that pierce through the skies.
Each moment a treasure, a glint in the dark,
Guiding us gently, igniting the spark.

Hints of Enchantment

In the rustle of leaves, a secret unfolds,
Hints of enchantment in stories retold.
Breezes that carry the scent of the night,
Guide us to realms where the spirits take flight.

With every soft chuckle, a spell is cast,
Echoes of laughter from shadows long past.
In glimmers of magic, we find our embrace,
Hints of enchantment in this sacred space.

Soft Embrace of Fading Light

Softly whispers twilight's glow,
As shadows dance in gentle flow.
The day concedes to night's caress,
In the stillness, we find rest.

Crickets sing a soothing tune,
Beneath the watchful, silver moon.
Each breath a sigh, each moment brief,
In fading light, we find relief.

Light's Breathe Upon the Surface

Morning breaks with tender grace,
A golden touch, a warm embrace.
Ripples shimmer, a gentle rise,
Reflecting dreams beneath the skies.

Whispers carried by the breeze,
Nature's song puts hearts at ease.
Each ray a bridge, a pathway clear,
In every glow, the world feels near.

Glimmers of Serenity in Between

In the pauses, calm prevails,
Where time reflects in silent trails.
Soft echoes linger, ever sweet,
Moments stitched where stillness meets.

Petals fall like whispered dreams,
Caught in sunlight's gentle beams.
Breath of peace, a quiet sigh,
In this space, our spirits fly.

Garden of Shifting Shades

Where colors blend and shadows roam,
In shifting light, we find our home.
Each petal tells a story rare,
In whispers soft, a fragrant air.

Beneath the arch of leafy boughs,
Time lingers slow, and silence bows.
A tapestry of life unfolds,
In every hue, a heart consoled.

Where Light Meets Shape

In shadows deep, they dance and play,
Forms emerge as night gives way.
Soft outlines kiss the dawn's embrace,
A harmony in time and space.

Whispers of color weave and flow,
Where edges blur, new visions grow.
Luminescence shows the way,
As light and shape begin to sway.

The Allure of Half-Light

In twilight's grasp, the world ignites,
Hints of gold in fading sights.
Silhouettes breathe in dusk's soft choir,
A magical spell we can't retire.

Misty veils wrap the night,
Echoes linger, soft and slight.
In shadows cast by the moon's glow,
A realm of dreams begins to grow.

Dreamscapes in Contrast

Between the light and dark we tread,
A canvas where our thoughts are spread.
Bold colors clash, yet softly blend,
In visions that never seem to end.

Scenes of night with splashes bright,
Alluring chaos in subtle flight.
A bridge between the now and then,
In silence found beyond the pen.

Fading Radiance

As day slips softly into dusk,
The last of warmth, a fleeting husk.
Embers dim, but hearts still glow,
In memories where love will flow.

Time spirals on, yet shadows stay,
In every breath, the light will play.
A tapestry of moments past,
In fading hues, our dreams hold fast.

The Melodies of Light and Dark

In shadows deep the whispers glide,
Soft echoes from the night reside.
A dance between the bright and dim,
Where secrets play on a fleeting whim.

The sun's embrace and moon's caress,
Compose a song of sweet finesse.
Each note a fleeting, tender spark,
A symphony of light and dark.

Cascades of Daylight

Golden rays on morning dew,
Awakening the world anew.
Each droplet sings a vibrant tune,
As day expands to meet the noon.

The trees in harmony and grace,
Dance gently in the sun's embrace.
A cascade of warmth that flows so free,
Illuminating all we see.

Elysian Lightplay

Amidst the fields where soft winds blow,
A tapestry of colors will show.
The light that filters through the leaves,
Creates a world where magic weaves.

Dancing shadows, laughter bright,
In a realm of pure delight.
Elysian dreams in every sight,
Radiating love, pure and light.

Tangled in Twilight

As dusk descends with hues of blue,
The day exhales, bidding adieu.
Whispers of night begin to call,
As day retreats to shadows tall.

Twilight dances on the edge of dreams,
Crafting a world where nothing seems.
In this serene and soft embrace,
All time melts into twilight's grace.

Fluttering Shadows in the Garden

In the garden where whispers play,
Butterflies dance, a soft ballet.
Petals flutter, kissed by the breeze,
Shadows linger among the trees.

Sunlight dapples the emerald ground,
As laughter of crickets hums around.
Each moment a treasure, fleeting, bright,
Nature's secrets revealed in light.

Daylight Reverie: A Tangled Tale

In the daylight, dreams intertwine,
Stories whispered, lost in time.
Voices echo in the soft glow,
Yet reality pulls, fast and slow.

Memories linger like autumn leaves,
Caught in whispers the heart believes.
In this reverie, I wander far,
Chasing shadows, tracing a star.

Between Radiance and Darkness

The dusk hangs softly, a velvet shroud,
Where secrets gather, veiled in crowd.
Stars emerge, like whispers of fate,
Drawing lines between love and hate.

In the twilight, choices unfold,
A tale of tempests, brave and bold.
Between the day and the night's embrace,
Hope lingers softly in empty space.

The Dance of Brightness and Gloom

In the ballroom where shadows waltz,
Light and dark spin, no faults.
Echoes of laughter, tears blend,
In this dance, we must transcend.

Colors clash in a vibrant swirl,
A tapestry woven, a dizzying whirl.
With each step, the heart takes flight,
In the bond of day, and the pull of night.

The Linger of Warmth

A gentle breeze whispers low,
As sun dips behind the snow.
Embers glow in twilight's breath,
Hues of love, a tender wreath.

Days of summer fade to gray,
Yet warmth in hearts will stay.
Memories wrapped in soft light,
Guide us through the chilly night.

Flickers of Dawn's Kiss

The horizon blushes bright,
Welcomed by the morning light.
Birds serenade the day anew,
Each note a promise bold and true.

With every flicker, shadows flee,
A dance of hopes, wild and free.
The world awakens, fresh and pure,
In dawn's embrace, we find our cure.

Radiant Veils

Softly draped in colors wide,
The world wears beauty like a bride.
A tapestry of hues so bright,
Whispering secrets in the light.

Through petals soft and skies so blue,
Radiant veils, each moment new.
They carry dreams on gentle wings,
In every breath, the joy it brings.

Beneath the Glistening Canopy

In silence sung by leaves above,
Nature weaves her threads of love.
Each star a gem in velvet night,
Guiding souls with tender light.

Beneath the glistening, vibrant show,
We find our path where wildflowers grow.
In this embrace, hearts intertwine,
Under the mountains, where shadows shine.

Glistening Echoes

In the forest deep and wide,
Where whispers of the past abide,
Glistening echoes softly play,
Beneath the waning light of day.

A song of leaves on gentle breeze,
Nature's rhythm, sweetly frees,
Dancing sparkles on the stream,
Caught in the web of twilight's dream.

Voices linger, shadows blend,
In twilight's grace, they twist and bend,
Memories weave like threads of gold,
Stories of the brave and bold.

As stars awaken in the night,
Glistening echoes take to flight,
Carrying tales lost in time,
In whispered notes, they softly rhyme.

Afterglow of Dreams

In the hush of closing day,
Where colors softly sway,
The afterglow begins to swell,
Whispers of a distant bell.

Dreams unfurl like petals bright,
Bathed in warm, enchanting light,
Each moment wrapped in gentle sighs,
Floating softly, love replies.

As the heavens paint the skies,
In a dance where beauty lies,
Every wish and hope takes flight,
Chasing shadows into night.

The world transforms with every hue,
Afterglow brings something new,
In this twilight's sweet embrace,
Hopes and dreams shall find their place.

Dappled Light Secrets

In the forest where the sunlight glows,
Dappled light in gentle throws,
Secrets hidden in the shade,
Whispers of the tales unsaid.

Leaves are dancing, shadows twirl,
Nature sings in softest whirl,
Every ray, a path to tread,
Leading hearts where dreams are fed.

Mysterious paths of time and space,
Where hope and wonder find their grace,
In every glimmer, life unfolds,
Dappled light, a story told.

Listen closely, hear the sound,
Of secrets waiting to be found,
In the embrace of nature's art,
Dappled light will warm the heart.

Golden Threads of Twilight

As day surrenders to the night,
Golden threads of fading light,
Stitch together earth and sky,
A tapestry where dreams can lie.

Whispers float on gentle winds,
A melody that softly spins,
In this moment, time stands still,
Hearts united with sheer will.

Twilight paints with hues so rare,
A canvas rich beyond compare,
Every thread, a wish we weave,
In golden glow, we dare believe.

Through the shadows, hope shall gleam,
In twilight's embrace, we dream,
Golden threads will light the way,
Guiding souls till break of day.

Shifting Radiance

In twilight's grasp, the colors blend,
A dance of hues that never end.
Soft whispers trace the evening sky,
As day and night begin to die.

The stars awake, their secrets bright,
In sapphire depths of velvet night.
A luminous touch on shadows cast,
Moments fleeting, too swift to last.

The Unseen Glow

Beneath the dark, a warmth resides,
In hidden corners, magic hides.
A gentle flicker, a tender spark,
  Breathing life into the stark.

The heart knows well what eyes can't see,
In silence, truths flow silently.
Each pulse, each beat, a secret told,
  Stories written in threads of gold.

Spectrum of Shadows

Shadows stretch in the fading light,
Bending forms, a fleeting sight.
Each shape a whisper, a fleeting thought,
In twilight's grip, illusions wrought.

Colors blend in the dusk's embrace,
Secrets stitched in time and space.
A world transformed in soft decay,
In shadows' arms, we drift away.

Shivering Glistens

Morning dew on grass does cling,
A crystal world where fairies sing.
Each droplet holds the sun's bright kiss,
A fleeting moment of pure bliss.

In nature's grasp, the cool air sways,
Shivering glistens, as daylight plays.
A dance of light on fragile blades,
A masterpiece where wonder fades.

The Caress of Light

A soft touch warms the skin,
Whispering secrets of the dawn.
Golden rays break the cold,
Inviting life to carry on.

In the quiet of morning's grace,
Shadows dance with hopeful hearts.
Nature wakes from its embrace,
Each moment, a work of art.

Tendrils of sun weave through trees,
Kissing petals in pure delight.
Filling the world with gentle ease,
In the caress of lingering light.

The day unfolds with vibrant hue,
Every color bursts to play.
A symphony of shades so true,
Guiding us along our way.

Where Glow Meets Gloom

In twilight's edge, shadows creep,
Fingers of night stretch and sway.
Yet, amidst the deep, there's a keep,
A glow that beckons to stay.

Stars twinkle like distant dreams,
Filling the void with a spark.
They whisper soft, or so it seems,
Illuminating paths in the dark.

Amidst the silence, a flicker shows,
A candle's flame sways in the breeze.
It dances gently where no light glows,
A beacon of hope, destined to please.

Where glow meets gloom, hearts collide,
Finding magic in the night.
Holding on, we won't divide,
In the mingling of dark and light.

Radiant Remnants

Last night's stars began to fade,
Leaving traces soft and bright.
The world awakens, unafraid,
Holding on to the remnants of light.

Echoes of dawn paint the sky,
Brushstrokes in hues of gold.
As daylight whispers oh-so-sly,
Tales of the night, quietly told.

The sun climbs high, embracing all,
While memories softly retreat.
In the beauty of nature's call,
Radiant remnants find their seat.

Each moment holds a flicker's dance,
Lingering warmth in the air.
Life's fleeting, yet we take the chance,
To cherish what time lays bare.

Dreams in Dimmed Light

In the hush of a whispering night,
Dreams take flight in subtle sway.
Cradled soft in dimmed light,
Inviting our thoughts to play.

Beneath a canopy of stars,
Imagination roams so free.
Journeying beyond the bars,
Into realms of mystery.

Faced with shadows, we softly tread,
In the dance of the moon's pale glow.
Embracing what the mind has bred,
Where thoughts and wishes flow.

With each breath, the night unfolds,
A tapestry of hope and dreams.
In dimmed light, our truth beholds,
The quiet magic of moonbeams.

Subtle Vibrance

In whispers soft, colors blend,
A dance of hues, where shadows mend.
The world adorned in quiet grace,
Subtle tones, a warm embrace.

Moments glow, like twilight's kiss,
A fleeting touch of gentle bliss.
Nature's song in vibrant sighs,
Life awakens, softly cries.

Beneath the tree, the petals fall,
Each one caught in nature's thrall.
In tender light, the day unfolds,
Stories whispered, yet untold.

And in the dusk, a promise lingers,
The canvas waits, as daylight fingers.
Subtle vibrance shall remain,
Echoed in the heart's refrain.

Illumination's Edge

A spark ignites at day's first light,
Mountains rise with radiant height.
The dawn unveils its golden thread,
Whispers of hope in colors spread.

Through forest paths where shadows wane,
Sunbeams dance on the window pane.
Each moment glows, a fleeting spark,
Illuminating paths once dark.

The sky ablaze with shades of blue,
Clouds drift softly, edged with hue.
Nature's brush paints all in sight,
Transforming darkness into light.

At twilight's call, the stars emerge,
A cosmic wave, a gentle surge.
Illumination holds us near,
Embracing all that we hold dear.

Blurred Horizons

Beyond the fields, where the sky fades,
A world awaits in soft cascades.
The edges blend, where colors merge,
Blurred horizons, a quiet surge.

Gentle whispers of the breeze,
Carrying tales among the trees.
In stillness, mysteries unfold,
A palette rich, a sight to behold.

Shapes dissolve, a dreamlike scene,
Where everything feels serene.
We wander through this painted land,
With open hearts and outheld hand.

Embracing moments, lost in time,
Each shadow plays a perfect rhyme.
Blurred horizons draw us near,
To realms of wonder, free from fear.

The Luminous Lattice

Threads of light weave through the night,
A tapestry, both bold and bright.
Stars align in intricate design,
A luminous lattice, so divine.

Each beam a story, softly spun,
Shining down on everyone.
In unity, they share their glow,
A cosmic dance that ebbs and flows.

The moonlight bathes the silent ground,
In every corner, beauty found.
Embrace the glow, take a chance,
Join the universe in its dance.

As dawn arrives with gentle grace,
The lattice fades, yet leaves a trace.
In hearts and minds, it lingers on,
A luminous thread that can't be gone.

Patterns of Light on Ancient Stone

Sunshine weaves on weathered stone,
Whispers of time, ancient and alone.
Shadows dance in gentle grace,
Marking stories time can't erase.

Mosses cling in emerald hues,
Nature's brush in varied views.
Each crack tells of seasons past,
A testament that holds steadfast.

As light shifts, the patterns change,
A silent art that feels so strange.
Moments captured by sun's embrace,
In the heart of this tranquil space.

Time stands still, the world awakes,
In every shadow, a memory shakes.
Patterns of light on stone unfold,
An ancient tale that must be told.

The Symphony of Illumination

Each ray a note in grand design,
Illumination flows divine.
The sun sets low, a golden hue,
Painting skies in vibrant blue.

Whispers of light in twilight's grip,
Where shadows gather, and dreamers slip.
A symphony plays in every beam,
Life awakens, a vibrant dream.

Stars emerge, a rhythmic spark,
Guiding souls through the dark.
Moonlit tones serenade the night,
In this dance of pure delight.

Each flicker tells a tale anew,
Of moments lived, of skies so blue.
The symphony swells, as night prevails,
In the heart of silence, magic sails.

Hiding in Brightness

In every gleam, a secret lies,
Behind the glow, a hidden prize.
Bright are the days, yet shadows creep,
Into the depths where whispers sleep.

Dancing lights, they lure the soul,
Yet beneath the brilliance, we seek whole.
For what is bright can oft conceal,
The heart's true joy, the wounds that kneel.

Amidst the cheer, a silent cry,
Self-hidden truths that pass us by.
Hiding in brightness, we wear a mask,
In search of light, we tend to bask.

But in the glow, there's room to find,
The love we seek, both raw and blind.
Embrace the shadow, the hidden part,
For in that place, lies the journey's heart.

Ethers of Warmth Beneath the Canopy

Beneath the leaves, a soft embrace,
Whispers of warmth in a secret place.
Dappled sunlight filters through,
A dance of shadows, a tranquil view.

Moss carpets the forest floor,
Nature's quilt forevermore.
In each rustle, a story shared,
Of lives entwined, of hearts that dared.

Ethers rise with fragrant breath,
In harmony, defying death.
The canopy holds space to grow,
Where time stands still, and love can flow.

Underneath the branches wide,
Peaceful spirits softly bide.
Ethers of warmth, a tender gift,
In the forest's heart, our souls we lift.

Whispered Reflections

In the quiet of the night,
Shadows dance with gentle light.
Whispers travel through the space,
Echoes linger, soft embrace.

Mirrored thoughts upon the stream,
Carried forth like a dream.
Fleeting glimpses, tender sighs,
Underneath the starlit skies.

Breezes weave a silver thread,
Stories shared, unspoken, spread.
Memories held in hearts so dear,
Whispered secrets, crystal clear.

Upon the dawn, reflections fade,
Yet the whispers serenade.
In each moment, truth will blend,
Whispered thoughts will never end.

Fatigued Glow

Beneath the weight of weary skies,
The sun dips low, a tired sigh.
Colors blend in softest gray,
The world around begins to sway.

Fading light with gentle grace,
Leaves a trace in every space.
Silent whispers of the day,
Creep upon the night's ballet.

In heavy hearts, the shadows grow,
Casting dreams in a faint glow.
Yet in the dark, hope finds a way,
To bring a spark, to light the fray.

Embers dance on fragile air,
A reminder, light is rare.
Though fatigue may claim the hour,
Within the gloom lies hidden power.

The Mystery of Half-Tones

In the realm of muted hue,
Colors hide and merge anew.
Between the dark and light they dwell,
A silent tale they long to tell.

Fleeting whispers, shadows play,
As shades of gray lead the way.
Not all is lost nor clearly seen,
In half-tones lies the in-between.

Gentle gradients, softest blend,
Mysteries that curves extend.
In every stroke, a secret lies,
Waiting still beneath the skies.

Embrace the blur, the unknown space,
Where joy and sorrow interlace.
In half-tones, beauty finds its voice,
Inviting heart and mind to rejoice.

Touch of Aurora

Dancing lights in velvet night,
Whispers of a dawn's delight.
Colors bleed in cosmic dance,
In every hue, a fleeting chance.

The touch of aurora paints the skies,
With gentle strokes that mesmerize.
A tender kiss on frosty air,
Revealing wonders beyond compare.

In twilight's grasp, the world does glow,
As dreams awaken, softly flow.
The night retreats, but holds its sway,
In the embrace of light's ballet.

A tapestry of hope unfurled,
A promise made, a new world swirled.
The touch of aurora, bold and free,
Ignites the heart, sets spirits free.

Traces of Aurora on the Ground

Colors cascade upon the earth,
Nature's brush strokes in rebirth.
Whispers of dawn in hues so bright,
Traces of magic fade from sight.

Gentle reminders of night's retreat,
Softly painted where shadows meet.
Each fleeting moment captured in time,
A dance of wonder, a silent rhyme.

Footprints of light upon the dew,
Echoes of dreams, a vivid view.
In the stillness, beauty unfurls,
As night relinquishes its pearls.

Glowing beneath the sky's embrace,
Silent reflections in a tranquil space.
Nature's palette, a soft surround,
Traces of aurora on the ground.

Fleeting Moments of Daylight's Kiss

Sunrise spills gold on the horizon,
A tender touch, life's sweet season.
Waves of warmth in soft caress,
Moments cherished, no less, no less.

Flashes of brilliance, brief but bright,
Daylight graces the world with light.
Soft shadows linger, dance and play,
Fleeting moments drift away.

Stories woven in the sun's embrace,
Time stands still in this cherished space.
Every heartbeat, a pulse of bliss,
Captured in daylight's gentle kiss.

As twilight draws the curtain low,
Memories spark, like fireflies' glow.
In the twilight, reflections persist,
Fleeting moments of daylight's kiss.

Light and Shade Dance

In the grove where shadows weave,
Soft whispers of light gently cleave.
Patterns shifting with each breath,
A beautiful play of life and death.

Branches sway in a soulful trance,
While sunlight and darkness sweetly dance.
The world spins on in a tranquil state,
Each movement a moment, a twist of fate.

Echoing laughter in the bright,
A balance held between wrong and right.
Nature's rhythm, a sacred chance,
Where light and shade forever dance.

As twilight embraces the fading day,
Shadows stretch long, not far away.
In this theater, life takes a stance,
Where light and shade forever dance.

Whispers of Radiance

In the quiet, a lullaby sings,
Echoes of light on hidden wings.
Glimmers dance, a soft embrace,
Whispers of radiance fill the space.

Starlight drips like silver dew,
Painting dreams in shades of blue.
Every glance a gentle spark,
Illuminating the encroaching dark.

Moments shimmer with fleeting grace,
As twilight paints the evening's face.
In stillness, a breath of joy,
Softly threading hope to deploy.

Beneath the veil of the quiet night,
Radiant whispers take their flight.
In the heart, a melody grows,
As dreams unfurl like the petals of a rose.

Whispers of Light and Shade

In the hush of twilight's breath,
Shadows dance with softest grace,
The world holds secrets close,
Light and shade embrace.

Beneath the boughs, a story weaves,
Of whispering leaves and gentle sighs,
Sunbeams flicker, softly fade,
As time and stillness rise.

Moments linger, time stands still,
As twilight paints the world anew,
In the silence, wisdom speaks,
Where light and shadow softly grew.

Dappled Dreams on the Forest Floor

Sunlight spills through emerald leaves,
Creating patterns, bright and bold,
A tapestry of fleeting dreams,
In dappled light, secrets unfold.

Mossy carpets whisper tales,
Of ancient roots and gentle streams,
Where time slows down and magic thrives,
Enveloped in nature's dreams.

Tiny critters scamper past,
While shadows play and branches sway,
In the forest's heart, so deep,
Wonders thrive in soft array.

Echoes of Radiance

The sun dips low, the horizon glows,
Painting skies in hues so bright,
Whispers echo on the breeze,
As day gives way to night.

In the twilight, calls unfold,
Stars awaken, one by one,
Each twinkle holds a story told,
Of journeys danced beneath the sun.

Time cascades in glowing streams,
Where past and present intertwine,
Echoes of radiance softly weave,
A tapestry divine.

When Dawn Dances with Dusk

When dawn first kisses sleepy land,
A blush of gold begins to spread,
The world awakens, hand in hand,
With subtle hues that gently tread.

As dusk arrives, the moment sighs,
In tranquil hues of purple and rose,
A dance of light 'neath fading skies,
Where day and night, in friendship close.

The whispers of the night unfold,
Against the lingering light's embrace,
In every heartbeat, stories told,
As dawn and dusk find their place.

Beyond the Radiance

In the hush of twilight's glow,
Whispers weave through branches slow.
Stars awaken, silent flight,
Guiding dreams into the night.

Clouds drift softly, kissed by light,
Carrying secrets of the night.
Where the shadows tenderly sway,
Beyond the radiance, drift away.

Ethereal Glimmers

Misty realms of silver dew,
Dancing softly, dreams accrue.
Each glimmer holds a story bright,
Painting visions into night.

Gentle breezes, secrets shared,
Eclipsing woes, bringing care.
In the quiet, whispers gleam,
Ethereal glimmers, lost in dream.

Twilight's Embrace

Underneath the fading light,
Day surrenders to the night.
Stars like lanterns softly bloom,
Chasing shadows, quiet gloom.

In the calm where silence lays,
Hearts entwined in time's soft haze.
In the stillness, hope's embrace,
Finding solace, twilight's grace.

Threads of the Day

Woven patterns, golden rays,
Threads of laughter, dance and play.
Moments linger, sweetly spun,
In the warmth of setting sun.

Echoes of the day persist,
Memories wrapped in twilight mist.
With every thread, a story found,
In the woven light, we're bound.

Fleeting Hues of Twilight

As daylight fades beyond the hills,
Shadows stretch across the fields.
Colors blend in gentle sighs,
Whispers of the night revealed.

Stars begin their quiet dance,
A tapestry of shimmering light.
The world holds its breath in trance,
Embracing the calm of night.

Clouds wear shades of violet and grey,
Painting stories in the sky.
Time slips softly away,
In this moment, we can fly.

Fleeting hues that softly blend,
Mark the close of day's sweet grace.
In twilight's arms, around the bend,
Life's beauty finds its resting place.

Veils of Luminous Secrets

A soft mist drapes the evening night,
Veils of secrets, softly spun.
Whispers linger in the twilight,
Promises made by the sun.

Moonlight weaves a silver thread,
Through branches swaying in the breeze.
In silence, dreams are gently fed,
Where shadows dance among the trees.

Each star holds a tale untold,
Of lovers lost and wishes dreamed.
In nights of magic, hearts unfold,
As fleeting moments, softly gleamed.

Secrets beckon from the dark,
Inviting those who dare to seek.
In whispered tones, there lies a spark,
Of truths that only night can speak.

The Gentle Touch of Day's Embrace

Morning dew like diamonds glows,
Upon the petals, soft and bright.
Sunrise paints the world in rose,
Awakening life with light.

Birds call out in joyful song,
As shadows flee from the dawn.
In this moment, all feels strong,
Hope renewed as night is gone.

A gentle breeze caresses skin,
While colors blossom, rich and warm.
Each heartbeat feels a new begin,
In nature's cradle, safe from harm.

The day unfolds, a tender grace,
With every heartbeat, life takes flight.
Embraced by warmth in time and space,
We find our peace in morning light.

Silhouettes in the Golden Glow

Figures dance against the sun,
Softly etched in fading light.
Memories wrapped, all but done,
Life is found in fleeting sight.

Laughter echoes through the air,
With shadows playing on the ground.
In this warmth, we find our care,
In this moment, love is found.

Golden rays stretch far and wide,
Kissing faces with a glow.
In togetherness, we abide,
As day turns soft from bright to low.

Silhouettes in hues of gold,
Creating dreams where we belong.
In this loving warmth so bold,
Our hearts will always sing along.

The Palette of Dusk

Colors blend in the evening sky,
A canvas where day bids goodbye.
Shadows stretch and softly play,
Whispers of night lead the way.

Violet hues paint the horizon,
As stars emerge, one by one.
The air is cool, the world at rest,
In dusk's embrace, we are blessed.

Gentle breezes start to sigh,
Crickets chirp their lullaby.
With every moment, colors shift,
In the fading light, spirits lift.

A palette rich with memories,
Of laughter shared beneath the trees.
In this twilight symphony,
We find our peace, we feel so free.

Glimmers and Haze

In morning mist, the light will break,
A dance of shadows, softly quake.
Glimmers shine through hazy trails,
Nature whispers as beauty prevails.

Softly glows the distant sun,
Chasing dreams where rivers run.
Each sparkle caught in dew's embrace,
A fleeting moment, a perfect grace.

The world adorned in silken hues,
While gentle winds carry the news.
Birds take flight with joyous calls,
In this wonder, the spirit enthralls.

Amidst the haze, a clarity blooms,
Awakening life in vibrant rooms.
As day unfolds, our hearts will soar,
Chasing glimmers, forevermore.

Shadows of Warm Embers

In the quiet of the night,
Soft embers glow, casting light.
Shadows dance upon the walls,
A warmth that lingers, softly calls.

Crackling fire, a gentle sound,
In the dark, solace is found.
Friends gather close, tales unfold,
In the flicker, memories told.

The scent of pine, sweet and strong,
Echoes of laughter, a timeless song.
A world outside may fade away,
In this warmth, we choose to stay.

Under starlit skies, we share,
Dreams whispered in the cooling air.
Embers fade, but hearts remain,
In shadows of love, we find no pain.

Light's Veiled Embrace

Morning breaks with a gentle grace,
Nature wakes in light's soft embrace.
Sunbeams filter through the leaves,
A tapestry that nature weaves.

Each ray a whisper, each glow a song,
In the heart of the forest, we belong.
With every step, the world unfolds,
A symphony of green and gold.

Misty mornings, a dance of dew,
Bathed in light, everything feels new.
The beauty found in every trace,
Is a gift from light's warm embrace.

As day advances, shadows play,
In the glow of the sun's ballet.
In every moment, find your space,
To cherish life in light's veiled embrace.

Dances of the Day's End

The sun dips low, the sky aglow,
Shadows stretch, as breezes flow.
Twilight whispers, soft and clear,
Embracing night, as stars appear.

Colors blend in sweet embrace,
Nature sighs, in tranquil grace.
Day's end brings a gentle song,
In stillness, we find where we belong.

The moon awakes, with silver beams,
Painting dreams, in gentle streams.
As fireflies dance, in the cool night air,
We feel their magic, everywhere.

So let us sway to evening's tune,
Under the watch of the radiant moon.
In the dances of the day that's done,
We find our peace, and we are one.

Murmurs in Sunlit Halls

In sunlit halls, where whispers play,
Dreams unfold in bright array.
Soft laughter chimes, like silver bells,
As stories weave their timeless spells.

The warmth of light, through windows gleams,
Filling hearts with hopeful dreams.
Each shadow dances, light and free,
Embracing all that's meant to be.

Footsteps echo on polished floors,
Memories linger, behind closed doors.
In every corner, life's tapestry,
Threads of joy and melancholy.

In sunlit halls, where time stands still,
We find our courage, we find our will.
We hold the moments, gentle and bright,
In the whispers of warm summer light.

Flickering Flickers

Flickering flames in the darkened night,
Dancing shadows, a fleeting sight.
Whispers of warmth, they softly call,
In their embrace, we feel so small.

Each flicker tells a tale untold,
Of dreams forgotten, of hearts so bold.
They quiver softly, like breathing air,
A dance of secrets, a precious flare.

In candlelight, the world slows down,
Lost in the glow, we wear our crown.
Time suspends, as moments blend,
Flickering memories that never end.

So let us gather, share our light,
In flickering comfort, on this quiet night.
For though the flame may wane and sigh,
In its warmth, our spirits fly.

The Glow Within Shadows

In silence deep, where shadows lie,
There blooms a glow that catches the eye.
A hidden spark in the darkest place,
Illuminating dreams with tender grace.

Through tangled paths, where fear may tread,
The glow within whispers, gently spread.
Guiding lost souls through nights of doubt,
Showing the way, when hope seems out.

Each flicker pulses, a heartbeat true,
Lighting the way, for me and you.
In the stillness of shadows, we can find,
The glow that exists in heart and mind.

So fear not the dark, nor the unknown,
For within the shadows, love has grown.
Embrace the light, let it be your guide,
In the glow within, we will abide.

The Invisible Embrace

In shadows deep, where whispers lay,
Silent bonds that softly sway,
Hearts entwined in a gentle grace,
Love's warmth felt in an unseen place.

Through tangled thoughts, the spirits dance,
In the stillness, a fleeting chance,
To find solace in quiet dreams,
Where every glance is more than it seems.

The night unfolds its velvet cloak,
Words unspoken, yet softly spoke,
In every heartbeat, a silent claim,
In this embrace, we are the same.

Though eyes may never meet the light,
Together we stand, lost in the night,
A world unseen, where souls ignite,
In invisible arms, we take flight.

Sunlit Reveries

Beneath the sky of azure hue,
The golden rays weave dreams anew,
Whispers of hope in the gentle breeze,
Carrying joys as sweet as these.

Fields of daisies stretch far and wide,
With laughter echoing, side by side,
Moments of magic in every glance,
In sunlight's embrace, we dare to dance.

Clouds drift by, like thoughts untold,
Stories of warmth in the air, behold,
Each sunbeam a note in a melon's song,
In this bright world, we all belong.

As twilight comes with a soft caress,
The day's sweet memories gently impress,
In the heart of dawn, we find our way,
In sunlit reveries, forever we stay.

Mirage of Half-Light

In the dusk where shadows play,
Whispers dance upon the fray.
Fading hues of gold and grey,
Time stands still, dreams drift away.

Half-lit visions softly blend,
Promises that fate will send.
Echoes linger, edges bend,
In this space, we find our mend.

Silhouettes of what might be,
Carried on a gentle sea.
With each breath, we long to see,
The truth hidden in the spree.

Caught between the night and day,
Secrets wrapped in soft decay.
In the twilight's warm array,
Hope still flickers, guiding sway.

Shimmering Paths

In the forest, moonlight spills,
Beneath the stars, lingering thrills.
Each step echoes, silence fills,
Walking through with whispered wills.

Branches sway with tales untold,
Every path a dream to fold.
Golden rays, the night unfolds,
A journey bright, a heart of gold.

Through the mist, the shadows weave,
Memories held, yet to believe.
With each twist, we learn to grieve,
The shimmering light we receive.

Paths converge and then depart,
Intertwined like every heart.
In this dance, we find our part,
A tapestry of souls impart.

Embrace of the Ember

In the dark, a fire glows,
Flickering warmth, time slows.
Crimson sparks in softness flows,
In this glow, our spirit grows.

Each ember tells a tale of old,
Of whispered dreams, secrets bold.
Wrapped in warmth, the night unfolds,
Together, we embrace the cold.

Through the flicker, futures gleam,
In the heartbeat, love's sweet dream.
In the silence, shadows seem,
To dance along like woven stream.

Within the fire's gentle sway,
Hope ignites with each new day.
In its embrace, we find our way,
A timeless bond, come what may.

Luminous Silhouettes

Underneath the starry sky,
Figures dance, they drift and fly.
Shadows cast as moments sigh,
In the night where dreams comply.

Each silhouette a story spun,
Chasing moments, one by one.
With each breath, the past we shun,
In the glow, new lives begun.

Softly glowing, hearts align,
In the night, your hand in mine.
Together, we boldly shine,
Echoes of a deep entwine.

Here we stand, time's gentle veil,
In this light, we shall prevail.
Luminous dreams, we will not fail,
As our spirits weave the tale.

Flares of Hope Underneath the Boughs

In the hush where silence grows,
Flickering light begins to pose.
Beneath the boughs, the whispers sway,
Stirring hearts that find their way.

The leaves can hold such dreams untold,
Flares of hope, bright and bold.
Nature weaves its tender thread,
Guiding souls where fears have fled.

Moments wrapped in leafy grace,
Sunlight dances, leaves embrace.
Tales of courage shape the air,
Beneath the boughs, love's answer fair.

In each shadow, a spark of light,
Flares of hope that pierce the night.
Finding strength in nature's art,
Underneath the boughs, we start.

Light-Sifting Dreams

Gentle beams slide through the haze,
Crafting worlds in a dreamy blaze.
Each glimmer holds a whispered tune,
Spinning dreams beneath the moon.

In the twilight, wishes play,
Light-sifting in a magical way.
Thoughts take flight on feathered wings,
Unraveling all that hope brings.

In dusk's embrace, the colors blend,
A symphony that seems to mend.
Hearts engage in quiet schemes,
With every breath, light-sifting dreams.

Chasing visions, hand in hand,
Together we'll make our stand.
As shadows shift, reality gleams,
In the heart of light-sifting dreams.

Kaleidoscope of Breaking Dawn

Morning whispers, colors blend,
A kaleidoscope, bright visions send.
Soft hues dance in a golden hue,
Awakening the world anew.

The sun unfurls its gentle rays,
Painting skies in vivid displays.
Each moment sparkles, rich and rare,
A breaking dawn beyond compare.

Birds take flight, a joyful spree,
Filling hearts with purest glee.
Within the warmth, dreams start to bloom,
In the light, we cast away gloom.

As shadows stretch, a promise grows,
In the dawn's glow, love freely flows.
We embrace the day, hand in hand,
Kaleidoscope of dreams so grand.

Enigmatic Play of Shadows

In the corners where sunlight fades,
Enigmatic shadows weave cascades.
Figures dance in twilight's breath,
Hidden stories, whispers of death.

Mysterious shapes twist and bend,
Playing games that never end.
In the darkness, a tale unfolds,
Secrets kept and truths untold.

Glimmers tease the watcher's mind,
In the play, illusions bind.
Every flicker, a moment's sigh,
Shadows beckon, spirits fly.

Within the night, the heart must dare,
To find the light hiding there.
In shadows' play, we find our way,
An enigmatic night to sway.

The Dance of Warmth

In the glow of the fading light,
Laughter echoes, hearts take flight.
Hands entwined, we swayed and spun,
Beneath the stars, two become one.

The embers spark a vibrant bloom,
Cocooned within this warm night's room.
Moments drip like honeyed grace,
In the dance, we find our place.

Whispers float on gentle air,
Each breath shared, a silent prayer.
The rhythm of joy, a tender thread,
In this dance, we're gently led.

As the night softly unfolds,
Secrets whispered, stories told.
With every step, our spirits soar,
In the dance of warmth, forevermore.

Hues of Serenity

In the quiet of the dawn,
Colors wake, the night is gone.
Pastel skies, a soft embrace,
Nature's art, a tranquil space.

Gentle waves kiss golden sand,
Footprints linger, hand in hand.
The breeze carries a soothing tune,
Underneath the watching moon.

Foliage dances in the light,
Shadows blend with pure delight.
Every hue, a calming balm,
In this world, we find our calm.

Time stands still, a breath we take,
In his serenity, our hearts awake.
Embraced by nature's gentle sway,
In these hues, we choose to stay.

Flickering Hope

A tiny spark in the dark night,
A glimmered promise, burning bright.
When shadows loom, and fears ignite,
Hope flickers on, a guiding light.

Through the storms and endless rain,
Resilience blooms from all the pain.
Like a candle's steady flame,
In fragile moments, hope remains.

With every setback, we rise anew,
In the night sky, stars break through.
Each flicker shouts, 'You are not lost,'
Hope's gentle hands, unwavering frost.

Let hearts be bold, let dreams unfold,
In the dark, we find our gold.
For every flicker fuels the fire,
With hope, we reach, we shall aspire.

Light Beneath the Leaves

Sunlight dances on the ground,
Among the trees, a sacred sound.
Whispers weave through branches high,
In this haven, spirits fly.

The rustling leaves compose a song,
Nature's chorus, vast and strong.
Beneath their shade, we find our peace,
In tender moments, worries cease.

Golden beams peek through the green,
Painting dreams where we've been.
In this light, our souls awake,
Connection deepens with each shake.

A tapestry of life unfolds,
In every shadow, stories told.
With every step beneath the trees,
We find our light, our hearts at ease.

Reflections of Warmth and Mystery

In the glow of the setting sun,
Whispers of shadows begin to run.
Lives intertwine with stories untold,
In the warmth, secrets unfold.

Eyes searching for what lies beneath,
Every glance, a stolen wreath.
Mysteries dance on the evening air,
Inviting hearts to dare and share.

Footsteps echo on cobbled stones,
Memory lingers, where the heart roams.
A gentle breeze carries our sighs,
In twilight's embrace, the truth lies.

Through the night sky, stars weave their light,
Illuminating dreams out of sight.
In the cool breeze, soft secrets hum,
As the day fades, new wonders come.

Chasing the Light Beyond the Trees

Beneath a canopy leafy and green,
Sunbeams dance, playful and keen.
Nature's chorus calls with delight,
As we run towards the fading light.

The path ahead twists and bends,
Carving tales that time transcends.
Branches sway, sharing their lore,
As we chase what we're searching for.

Whispers of the past linger still,
In every rustle, the air we fill.
Moments blend like colors in a dream,
Life's vibrant canvas, a flowing stream.

In the twilight glow, shadows grow long,
Accompanying us, an ancient song.
With every step, we break the night,
Chasing the magic, chasing the light.

Magic in the Flicker of Moments

In quiet corners where life resides,
Magic lingers, where time divides.
A smile exchanged, a glance that glows,
Moments flicker, as the heart knows.

Captured time in a breathless pause,
Every heartbeat without a cause.
Laughter echoes, sweet and rare,
Fleeting glimpses of love laid bare.

Stars appear when the daylight wanes,
Illuminating thoughts in refrain.
The evening breeze carries a sigh,
As dreams awaken beneath the sky.

In the stillness, time bends and sways,
Magic resides in the simplest ways.
Treasured memories wrapped in light,
Flickering softly, through the night.

Secrets Unraveled by Afternoon Rays

Afternoon sun drapes softly on skin,
Revealing places where shadows begin.
Beneath the warmth, whispers arise,
Every story adorned with guise.

Golden lights cast a delicate hue,
Illuminating paths where dreams pursue.
In gardens where laughter intertwines,
Secrets unfold with the passing signs.

Captured in rays that gently sway,
Moments continue, come what may.
Time dances lightly, a fleeting dream,
In the heart's quiet, secrets redeem.

Through the haze of a day grown old,
Life reveals truths waiting to be told.
As shadows recede with the setting sun,
Afternoon whispers, weaves us as one.

Shadows in Silken Hues

Whispers dance in twilight's grace,
A tapestry of light's embrace.
Soft silhouettes in gentle sway,
Reveal the night, where dreams will play.

Veils of mist in sultry air,
Cascading stars beyond compare.
Each fading hue a story told,
In shadows bright, our hearts unfold.

Moonlight spills on dewy ground,
Silken threads where love is found.
Glimmers merge in secret sighs,
As time dissolves beneath the skies.

Lost in the glow of woven night,
We find our peace in quiet light.
Each shadow holds a memory dear,
In silken hues our dreams appear.

The Echo of Dappled Light

Under canopies of leafy grace,
Soft whispers find their secret place.
Dappled light in playful streams,
Mirrors the song of waking dreams.

Nature's breath, a gentle sigh,
Where sunbeams touch and shadows lie.
Every flicker, a heartbeat's call,
In this embrace, we find it all.

Petals shimmer in sunlight's glow,
As soft winds of memory blow.
The echo of laughter, bright and clear,
In dappled light, we draw them near.

A dance of patterns on the ground,
In every moment, magic found.
Through every shade, we leap and twirl,
In sacred circles, our spirits whirl.

Twilight's Lullaby

In twilight's arms, the world slows down,
A cradle formed from dusk's soft crown.
Gentle breezes hum a tune,
As stars awaken, one by one.

The sky blushes in shades of wine,
Painting dreams along the line.
Each whisper carries hopes anew,
In twilight's glow, the heart breaks through.

Night's velvet cloak wraps tight and warm,
Comfort found in its embrace charm.
Crickets sing their symphony,
A lullaby for you and me.

Rest in the stillness, close your eyes,
As moonbeams dance through velvet skies.
In twilight's arms, we drift away,
To dream of love till break of day.

Crepuscular Whispers

In the fading light, secrets thrive,
Where shadows stretch and silence arrive.
Whispers float on the evening air,
Painting tales of dreams laid bare.

Crisp leaves rustle, a soft refrain,
Echoes of laughter, love's sweet gain.
Fingers of dusk weave through the trees,
Harmonizing with the sighing breeze.

Stars peek through the twilight's veil,
Guiding lost souls with a subtle trail.
In every crease of the dimming light,
Crepuscular whispers speak of night.

The world at rest, in shadows steep,
Cradles the dreams that softly creep.
In this hush, our spirits meet,
Entwined in night, our hearts complete.

Milton Keynes UK
Ingram Content Group UK Ltd.
UKHW022222251124
451566UK00006B/84